COLOSSIANS AND PHILEMON

Living Word BIBLE STUDIES

COLOSSIANS AND PHILEMON

Continue to Live in Him

KATHLEEN BUSWELL NIELSON

P&R PUBLISHING
P.O. BOX 817 • PHILLIPSBURG • NEW JERSEY 08865-0817

Printed in the United States of America

CONTENTS

Contents

FOREWORD

Why study the Bible? And if we do study the Bible, how should we study it?

Maybe the best way to answer these questions is by seeing what the Bible says about itself.

The Bible says that it is the very Word of God, breathed out by the Holy Spirit (2 Tim. 3:16–17). The one true and living God speaks to us in every word on every page. And we should reverently and joyfully recognize our awesome privilege as direct recipients of divine revelation. Therefore, we should believe that as we read and study the Bible we are hearing the voice of God. Then we will be worthy of the commendation that the apostle Paul gave to the Thessalonians: "We also thank God constantly for this, that when you received the word of God, which you heard from us, you accepted it not as the word of men but as what it really is, the word of God" (1 Thess. 2:13).

The Bible also says that the God-given Word was written by real human beings, who wrote under the direction of God the Holy Spirit (see 2 Peter 1:21). The Bible was written for people like us, by people like us. Furthermore, these divinely inspired authors claimed to write with special care and the best efforts of their literary skill. For example, the writer of Ecclesiastes said that he "taught the people knowledge, weighing and studying and arranging many proverbs with great care," and that he "sought to find words of delight, and uprightly he wrote words of truth" (Eccl. 12:9–10).

We should read the Bible, therefore, both as a divine book and as a human book. This means recognizing and understanding the conventional literary forms in which the Bible is written: stories, poems, lists, hymns, genealogies, visions, laments, historical records, and so forth. It means that as we read, we should find pleasure and take delight in the Bible's beauty, simplicity, and majesty. It also means that we should take as much care to study the Bible as the original authors took to write it, paying close attention to every word that was carefully chosen to fit into its proper context.

The Bible claims further that the Word of God is something we need to live. Jesus said it like this: "Man shall not live by bread alone, but by every word that comes from the mouth of God" (Matt. 4:4; cf. Deut. 8:3). In other words, we need God's Word as much or even more than we need our daily bread. Therefore, we should read and study the Bible every day as if our lives depended upon it.

To be more specific, the Bible says that it has the life-giving power to bring us into a saving relationship with Jesus Christ. The sacred writings of Scripture "are able to make you wise for salvation through faith in Christ Jesus" (2 Tim. 3:15). The saving wisdom of Scripture is not limited to one part of the Bible or another but holds true for every book in the Old and New Testaments. What John said about his gospel is really true about the whole Bible: "These are written so that you may believe that Jesus is the Christ, the Son of God, and that by believing you may have life in his name" (John 20:31; cf. Luke 24:25–27).

As we read and study the Bible we should look to see Jesus on every page. The Savior expected in the prophets is exhibited in the gospels, explained in the epistles, and exalted in the Revelation. As we read these Scriptures by faith, therefore, we come into a personal saving knowledge of Jesus Christ.

What else does the Bible say about itself? It says that God's Word is a lamp to our feet and a light to our path (Ps. 119:105). In other words, the Bible shows us the way to go in life. In fact, the Bible tells us everything we need for godly thinking and holy living: every word of Scripture is "profitable for teaching, for reproof, for correction, and for training in righteousness, that the man of God may be competent, equipped for every good work" (2 Tim. 3:16–17). The Bible is the most useful book ever written. As we read, therefore, we should be looking for practical truth that will make a difference in what we think, what we say, and what we do in every situation in life.

This study guide will give you a helpful method for studying the Bible in all the right ways. It will encourage you in the daily reading, meditation, and memorization of Scripture. It will help you to be serious and systematic about studying the Bible for yourself. It will ask you questions that help you see the literary structure, the Christ-centered meaning, and the practical implications of what you are reading. It will give you growing skill and confidence in understanding the Bible, while at the same time helping you make progress in personal holiness and deepening your love for God the Father, God the Son, and God the Holy Spirit. And it will help you do all of this in relationship with other members of your spiritual family—your brothers and sisters in the church.

Colossians and Philemon are richly rewarding letters to study. In Colossians, the apostle Paul celebrates the absolute supremacy of Jesus Christ, corrects some soul-destroying errors in theology, and teaches us how to live for Christ in our daily relationships. In Philemon he addresses a delicate interpersonal conflict in the church, helping us see how to honor God in restoring a relationship.

May the same Holy Spirit who first revealed these words to the apostle enable you to understand what you read, to find joy in what you study, and to return the glory to God by the way that you live.

Philip Graham Ryken

A PERSONAL WORD
FROM KATHLEEN

I began to write these Bible studies for the women in my own church group at College Church in Wheaton, Illinois. Under the leadership of Kent and Barbara Hughes, the church and that Bible study aimed to proclaim without fail the good news of the Word of God. What a joy, in that study and in many since, to see lives changed by the work of the Word, by the Spirit, for the glory of Christ.

In our Bible study group, we were looking for curriculum that would lead us into the meat of the Word and teach us how to take it in, whole Bible books at a time—the way they are given to us in Scripture. Finally, one of our leaders said, "Kathleen—how about if you just write it!" And so began one of the most joyful projects of my life: the writing of studies intended to help unleash the Word of God in people's lives. The writing began during a busy stage of my life—with three lively young boys, and always a couple of college English courses to teach—but through that stage and every busy one since, a serious attention to studying the Bible has helped keep me focused, growing, and alive in the deepest ways. The Word of God will do that. If there's life and power in these studies, it is simply the life and power of the Scriptures to which they point. It is ultimately the life and power of the Savior who shines through all the Scriptures from beginning to end. How we need this life in the midst of every busy and non-busy stage of our lives!

I don't think it is just the English teacher in me that leads me to this conclusion about our basic problem in Bible study these days: we've forgotten how to *read*! We're so used to fast food that we think we should be able to drive by the Scriptures periodically and pick up some easily digestible truths that someone else has wrapped up neatly for us. We've disowned that process of careful reading . . . observing the words . . . seeing the shape of a book and a passage . . . asking questions that take us into the text rather than away from it . . . digging into the Word and letting it speak! Through such a process, guided by the Spirit, the Word of God truly feeds our souls. Here's my prayer: that, by means of these studies, people would be further enabled to read the Scriptures profitably and thereby find life and nourishment in them, as we are each meant to do.

In all the busy stages of life and writing, I have been continually surrounded by pastors, teachers, and family who encourage and help me in this work, and for that I am grateful. The most wonderful guidance and encouragement come from my husband, Niel, whom I thank and for whom I thank God daily.

May God use these studies to lift up Christ and his Word, for his glory!

INTRODUCTION

Welcome to a study of Colossians and Philemon. Our goal will be to read, understand, and apply these two New Testament epistles. These are not simply beautiful and fascinating letters written during the first remarkable years of growth in the early church; these are the inspired, authoritative Word of God. The same Spirit who inspired these words can teach us what they mean and show us how to apply them to our lives. As we study, may the Word of God be truly living and active in our hearts and in our lives.

BACKGROUND OF PAUL AND THE CHURCH AT COLOSSAE

Colossians and Philemon are two of Paul's "prison epistles"—letters written while he was imprisoned, probably in Rome, around AD 60. He was bound in chains, he explained, "because of the hope of Israel" (Acts 28:20)—that is, because he preached the gospel of Jesus the promised Lord Christ. The Lord Jesus had appeared to Paul (then Saul) on the Damascus road, appointing him "as a servant and witness to the things in which you have seen me and to those in which I will appear to you" (Acts 26:16). The Lord had declared him "a chosen instrument of mine to carry my name before the Gentiles and kings and the children of Israel" (Acts 9:15). So the persecutor Saul became the persecuted apostle Paul, who never stopped carrying the name of the Lord Jesus Christ, no matter how he suffered for doing so.

One result of Paul's faithful witness was the salvation of a whole group in Colossae through a Colossian man named Epaphras, who was evidently converted under Paul's preaching in Ephesus and who then carried the gospel back home to Colossae, just eighty miles away. A strong church grew in Colossae, a small town in the Lycus river valley (in modern-day Turkey), near the larger cities of Laodicea and Hierapolis (see Col. 4:13). These towns were all directly inland from Ephesus, and their inhabitants would have been included in "all the residents of Asia . . . both Jews and Greeks" who "heard the word of the Lord" through Paul's preaching in Ephesus (Acts 19:10).

Now, later, Paul in prison receives a visit from Epaphras, hears of the Colossian church and its struggles, and writes them this loving letter. At the same time, he writes a personal letter to a Colossian believer named Philemon, sending that letter by the hand of Philemon's own runaway but now returning slave.

BACKGROUND OF THE CHURCH THREATENED BY FALSE TEACHING

Paul tells the Colossians that, as they have received Christ, so they must walk in Christ, who is fully sufficient—not only as Savior but also as Creator and Ruler of the whole world and everyone in it, forever and ever. Some false teachers in the early church were challenging the sufficiency of Christ, as we shall see. Just as in our world today, Christians in the early church faced a swirl of popular but heretical philosophies and religious views threatening to corrupt the pure message of the gospel of Jesus Christ. Some see Paul's warnings as targeting the early stages of Gnosticism, which eventually grew into a widely accepted heresy asserting the availability of a special knowledge beyond the knowledge of Christ. (The Greek word *gnosis* means "to know.") The various heresies of the day, against which Paul taught, made assertions such as the following:

- the existence of an elite few with special spiritual status, either through a superior knowledge or through adherence to certain rules or rituals.
- a superior wisdom, mysterious and hidden from most. Only a few could reach perfection.
- the importance of spirituality. Physical matter was either unimportant or evil. Such views led either to sinful license or to legalistic rules and regulations—as well as to a denial of the incarnation.
- the existence of many complicated levels of invisible spiritual powers, both good and evil. Some false teachers offered special knowledge of the evil powers and special means of protection from them.

Such false teaching sounds remarkably similar to many ideas coming at us in today's world, and perhaps even in today's church. The message of Colossians is relevant and alive in many ways.

METHODS OF STUDY

As we read and study God's Word, we will use certain basic Bible study methods, summarized just before chapter 1 in a section called "Studying a Book of the Bible." The primary goal is to understand and apply Colossians and Philemon, but one important related goal of this study is to help each participant further develop the ability to use these methods independently. It will be helpful to read and think through the outline of study methods so that you can watch for them and use them with awareness. The questions in this study will lead you through these methods (not always in the same order), asking you to try them out, encouraging your thoughtful interaction with the text. Finally, in the last lesson, on Philemon, you will be asked to work through these study methods by yourself—just you and the text in front of you. What a joy for each of us to be developing more and more of an ability to take up the Word of God, read it, understand it, and apply it.

This can happen only under the direction of the Holy Spirit. We need God's Spirit to understand God's Word in the way that he intends. Let us approach the Scriptures with humility and reverence, for they are the word of the Lord to us. Let us approach them with prayer, asking God by his Spirit to fill us with "the riches of full assurance of understanding" found only in our Lord Jesus Christ.

STUDYING A BOOK
OF THE BIBLE

I. Simply *read* the book through several times, making initial *observations*.

II. *Ask questions** about the book.
    1. Why is this text here?
       • In other words, identify the main point, or *theme*, of the book.
       • Look for a *theme verse* or verses that capture the book's main point.
    2. Why does it say what it says in the way that it says it?
       • Consider first the *original recipients* of the book and how they would have understood it.
       • Examine the book's *organization*, or shape: how do the different parts work together to support the main theme?
       • Find *key words* and determine their meaning and significance in the book.
       • Observe the book's *literary style* and the way in which that style contributes to the meaning.

* The five general questions have been suggested by Rev. Dick Lucas in teaching workshops at College Church in Wheaton, Illinois.

3. How does this text point us to Jesus?
   - Discover how, even indirectly, this book supports and develops the *Bible's main theme* of God's redeeming a people, through Jesus Christ for his own glory.
4. What are the surprises in this book?
   - Continually look to *notice* and *learn* what you didn't know or expect.
5. What is the application?
   - Identify *specific personal applications.*

III. *Study shorter sections* in detail, asking the following questions.
   1. What is the main idea here?
   2. What questions does the text make me ask?
   3. How does this section connect with verses before and after?
   4. How is this section organized?
   5. What key words do I find?
   6. How does this section support the book's main theme?
   7. What other Scriptures shed crucial light on these verses?
   8. How does this section apply to me?

Lesson 1

MEETING A NEW BOOK

DAY ONE—JUST READING!

Before we approach the study of Colossians in more detail, let's read it! There is no better starting point than the text itself—a letter from the apostle Paul to the church in Colossae. (See the introduction for further background.) For this first day, read the book straight through in one sitting, which should take about twenty to thirty minutes. Do not stop in parts that seem difficult; we'll come back! Today's goal is to get a sense of the whole.

But wait . . . before beginning, speak to the Lord God who gave us this book, and ask him to teach you what it means, through his Holy Spirit who inspired it and who even today brings it to life in our minds and hearts.

DAY TWO—GETTING THE MAIN POINT

1. Today, have not a read-through but a slightly briefer look-through, again of the entire book. This time, as you make your way through the text, ask yourself what

Paul mainly seems to be after as he writes this epistle. Can you begin to identify a central theme that works its way through the whole book? Write down at least one or two possibilities.

2. Consider Colossians 2:6–7 as theme verses for this book.

   a. How might you sum up the message of these two verses?

   b. In what ways do these verses relate to what you've read in the book as a whole?

c. The title of this study was taken from an older translation, which rendered Colossians 2:6: "continue to live in him." The Greek verb here is literally "to walk": the verse tells us to "walk in him." How is this more literal rendering helpful and important?

d. If these verses do capture the book's main message, in what ways might you foresee and pray that this study of Colossians will apply to you?

DAY THREE—FINDING THE SHAPE

Every book has a shape, doesn't it—some organization that moves it on from the start to finish? Different readers find slightly different ways of finding order in a book like this; see what you can discover by looking at the text.

1. Giving one more look-through of the entire book, what general observations would you make concerning the way it develops, from beginning to end? Try to ignore the editors' paragraph breaks, chapter divisions, and headings, which were not in the original Greek text.

2. If you had to divide the book into two parts, using the theme verses (Col. 2:6–7) as a thematic guide, how might you do it?

3. What further sections or divisions of this book might you identify, between the introductory greetings (Col. 1:1–8) and the final greetings (Col. 4:7–18)?

Day Four—The Writer's Purpose for Us

Having gained an overview of this letter, its main message, and its general shape, we should ask at the start: what is the purpose of this book for us, in the whole scope of God's great biblical revelation? Paul states clearly his main purpose for those to whom he writes (Col. 2:2–4).

1. First, who are the ones for whom Paul wishes his purpose to be accomplished? See Colossians 2:1.

2. Some versions of Colossians 2:2 make it sound like there are several different (and confusing!) purposes. In the original language, there is only one "in order that"—and it's the first one: "that their hearts may be encouraged." The rest of the verse explains the nature of this encouragement with phrases that pile one on top of another to reach the climax: Christ.

   a. What do these rich phrases in Colossians 2:2 tell us about the kind of encouragement Paul is after?

   b. How does Colossians 2:3 explain and complete verse 2?

   c. According to these verses, what does it mean to know Christ?

3. Colossians 2:4 adds a further "in order that" for this letter. How will the purpose of Colossians 2:2–3 insure the purpose of verse 4?

Colossians' message will emphasize the reality and the treasure of all that is ours in Christ, if we have received him for who he is—and Paul will make clear who is this one in whom we are to put our faith. Continuing to know him more and to live in him faithfully is everything we need. May Paul's message truly strengthen and encourage our hearts.

Day Five—Prayer

How amazing to think that Paul wrote this letter not only for the churches of his day but for us as well, through the inspiration of the Holy Spirit. Take a few minutes to pray that this book of Colossians will accomplish in your life the purpose for which it was intended.

Lord God, as I study this book you have inspired and preserved, would you encourage my heart, according to your truth. Knit together in love those of us who study. May we together know more and more of the riches of full assurance of understanding found in Christ. May we plumb God's mystery, which has been revealed in Christ. Thank you for giving us your only Son, the Lord Jesus, in whom are hidden all the treasures of wisdom and knowledge.

May I take the message of Colossians to heart, knowing what it means not only to have received Christ Jesus the Lord but also to walk in him, rooted and built up in him, established in the faith and abounding in thanksgiving.

In Christ I pray. Amen.

Notes for Lesson 1

Lesson 2 (Col. 1:1–14)

PLUNGING IN . . .
WHO, WHAT, AND HOW?

DAY ONE—LOOKING AT THE PEOPLE

First, let's get straight the main characters involved in this letter. From the first eight verses, write down everything you know about these people and their relationships to each other.

1. Paul (Note: "Apostle" comes from the Greek verb "to send." An apostle of Christ was one sent out, commissioned by him, and one who had witnessed the resurrected Christ [Act 1:21–22].)

2. The ones in Colossae to whom he writes

3. Epaphras (See also Col. 4:12–13.)

DAY TWO—LOOKING AT THE LORD

Do you experience the kind of connection to people evidenced in these first verses? Many people today long for this sort of knitting together with others. Such connection does not happen naturally; as this book shows, it grows from the presence and working of the supernatural in people's hearts.

1. First, let's find out, from Colossians 1:1–14, everything we can learn about Jesus, the one who is at the center of this letter. Even the names given him are significant in telling us who he is. Right away (and repeatedly) he's called "Christ," which is the Greek version of the Old Testament "Messiah"—literally, "anointed one." Anointing in Old

Testament times referred to the symbolic pouring of oil on the head of the king of Israel. What does this name "Christ" tell us about Jesus?

2. Jesus is also called "Lord" (Col. 1:3), meaning "ruler." We'll see more of what this means as we read on, but at this point, according to Colossians 1:10, what should be our attitude toward Jesus the Lord?

3. A ruler king has to have a kingdom. From Colossians 1:12–14, list all that we can know about Jesus' kingdom.

4. Let's look at the passage again, this time to see God the Father who sent this beloved Son. Write down all that you can learn about God from Colossians 1:1–14.

DAY THREE—LOOKING AT THE GOSPEL

1. On day 2, we were already beginning to study the gospel—literally, the "good news." What is the gospel, and what can we know about it, according to Colossians 1:3–8?

2. One of Paul's clearest statements on the gospel is found in another of his letters, 1 Corinthians 15:1–4. What are the important elements of the gospel's message, according to these verses?

3. In New Testament times, as today, all kinds of people were trying to preach distorted versions of the one true gospel taught by the apostles and found in the Scriptures. In 1 Corinthians 15:2 and Colossians 1:23, Paul encourages Christians to do what with the true gospel, once they have received it?

4. Look again at our theme verses, Colossians 2:6–7. How might you sum up the message of those verses in terms of the gospel?

5. Have you received Christ Jesus as Lord—that is, have you believed the gospel? Write down for yourself where you presently stand in relation to the gospel.

DAY FOUR—LOOKING AT PAUL'S PRAYER

1. Paul's prayer for the Colossians begins with "and so" in Colossians 1:9. To what is Paul referring here? What is the logical connection between what he has said and what he is about to say?

2. As you read through Colossians 1:3–14, what do you notice about the way in which Paul prays for the Colossian believers?

3. Read Colossians 1:9–12 carefully, and then fill in

   a. the main request Paul makes of God for the Colossians (Col. 1:9).

   b. the desired outcomes of this request being answered.

   c. your observations concerning this prayer.

4. How might Paul's prayer for the Colossians challenge you to pray differently for sisters and brothers in Christ?

DAY FIVE—LOOKING BACK

1. As you reread this week's passage, Colossians 1:1–14, look for the way the gospel of Jesus Christ defines these believers' past, their present, and their future.

   a. What has happened to them in the past?

   b. What is happening in the present?

c.   What are they certain will happen in the future?

2. What things compete with Christ to define your past, your present, and your future? How might you increasingly see your life shaped by the gospel of Jesus Christ?

Notes for Lesson 2

Lesson 3 (Col. 1:15–23)

WHO IS THIS JESUS?

As Paul begins the main body of his letter, he lays the necessary foundation for walking in Jesus by addressing the question of just who he is. This lesson focuses us on Christ Jesus—who he is, what he has done, and what this means to us.

DAY ONE—WHO CHRIST IS

1. Colossians 1:15–20, perhaps the most exalted passage in the whole letter, reveals to us the grand mystery of who Jesus is. Before digging into the individual phrases, read these verses through several times, and then write a sentence explaining the main thrust of this passage.

2. We've already seen Jesus called the Son of God (Col. 1:13). What parts of today's passage (specifically Col. 1:15–20) clarify the relation of the Son to the Father, and how?

3. Think on the mystery of the incarnation, that Jesus is God come down to us in all his fullness. Write down any responses and implications that come to your mind.

Day Two—More of Who Christ Is

1. The "firstborn" for centuries was understood to be the honored son who received and took charge of the inheritance from the father. What little three-letter word do you find repeated again and again in Colossians 1:15–20? Locate the phrases where this word occurs, and explain what it tells us about Christ the firstborn.

2. "All creation" (Col. 1:15) leads us directly into Paul's discussion of Christ the Creator. Write down everything you can learn in Colossians 1:16–17 about Christ the Creator and his relationship to his creation.

3. It is important to see that Scripture consistently teaches the clear message of who Jesus is. As you carefully read the following passages, what do you find that confirms and clarifies what we've seen about Jesus so far?

a. Hebrews 1:1–3

b. John 1:1–4, 14

DAY THREE—WHAT CHRIST HAS DONE

The passage focuses in, moving from Christ ruling over all creation to Christ ruling over a new creation: his people, the church.

1. What does the picture in the first sentence of Colossians 1:18 lead you to understand about Christ's relationship to his church? See also Colossians 2:19.

2. The second part of Colossians 1:18 refers to Christ's resurrection from the dead. What does the fact that Christ was the first one resurrected to eternal life mean to us, both now and in the future? Before answering, read 1 Corinthians 15:12–23, as well as Colossians 1:18.

3. Colossians 1:19–20 summarizes Christ's role in God's great redemptive plan. Taking account of each phrase, make a list or outline of observations about what God was pleased to do for us through Jesus Christ.

DAY FOUR—WHAT CHRIST HAS DONE FOR US

Now Paul addresses the Colossian believers more directly as part of the body that Christ rules. We can take these verses personally, as fellow members of that same body.

1a. What key idea in Colossians 1:20 is explained and developed in Colossians 1:21–22?

b. "Reconciliation" is a story of before and after. Find the key transition words and the key concepts for the before and after in Colossians 1:21–22.

2a. What words in Colossians 1:21 help you better understand our sinful condition? How?

b. Is this alienation from God because of sin a difficult concept for people to accept? Why or why not?

3. Some of the most common false teachings challenging believers in the early church were forms of Gnosticism, a view holding that material things were evil and that special spiritual knowledge was available to a certain elite. (See the introduction.) Considering this background, what do you note about the way Paul chooses to say what he says in Colossians 1:21–22?

4. Read carefully through Ephesians 2:1−5, also written by Paul. Note what similar emphases you find in the before and after, as well as what additional insights you gain into this story of reconciliation.

Day Five—Continue in This Gospel

1. According to Colossians 1:23, what things are crucial for us to do and know in relation to this gospel of Jesus Christ that Paul has been writing about?

2. The concern for continuing and not shifting (Col 1:23) may take us again to Colossians 2:6–7. How does the passage studied this week (Col. 1:15–23) connect to those theme verses?

3a. What do you think makes it difficult for you to "continue in the faith, stable and steadfast, not shifting from the hope of the gospel"?

b. What, specifically, from this week's passage, can encourage your heart to live steadfastly and unswervingly according to the gospel of Jesus Christ?

Notes for Lesson 3

Lesson 4 (Col. 1:24–2:5)

INTO THE HEART OF PAUL

As Paul reflects on the gospel's transformation of the Colossians, he rejoices in his own participation in God's saving purposes. Look through this week's passage and note Paul's use of "I." He is opening up his heart. Our goal will be to look into the apostle's heart and learn—from his suffering, his servanthood, and his battle against falsehood.

DAY ONE—PAUL'S SUFFERING

1. Colossians 1:24 is an amazing and much-discussed verse! Let's recall, first, the ways in which Paul suffered for the sake of the gospel. Read 2 Corinthians 6:4–10.

2. Paul's rejoicing in his suffering relates to what he says in the rest of Colossians 1:24. As you read this verse carefully, what questions does it make you ask?

3. The rest of Scripture teaches clearly that there is no defect or lack in Jesus' atoning work on the cross; his death is fully sufficient, a perfect sacrifice for our sins. What, then, is lacking? John Piper has connected Colossians 1:24 to Philippians 2:30, the only other verse that puts the same two Greek words together.* The Philippians' gifts to Paul were fixed and ready, but Epaphroditus was the one who had to deliver them in person. He came representing the Philippians, bringing the gifts to Paul in Rome, enduring great suffering and risking his life—as Paul puts it, "to complete what was lacking in your service to me." Read Philippians 2:25–30, and then go back to Colossians 1:24. How do you think Philippians might help interpret Colossians here?

* Chapel address, Wheaton College, February 11, 1998

4. Paul fills up in his "flesh," through suffering, that which is still lacking in regard to Christ's afflictions. Why can Paul rejoice in his sufferings, as he says in Colossians 1:24? See also Philippians 3:10.

DAY TWO—PAUL'S SERVANTHOOD

1. Paul's rejoicing in his suffering will become clearer as we see more clearly his commission as a minister of the gospel. Write down everything you can observe about this commission (Col. 1:23–25).

2. Read the following list of verses. What do they tell us about Paul's commission "to make the word of God fully known"?

- Colossians 1:26–27

- Acts 9:15

- Acts 1:8

- Psalm 67

- Genesis 12:1–3

3. Find two other places in Colossians where the word "fullness" or "fully" is used. How do these other uses shed light on what it means "to make the word of God fully known"?

4. How does Colossians 1:27 finally explain this "mystery"? What do you think the final phrase of verse 27 means?

DAY THREE—
PAUL'S STRUGGLE AGAINST FALSEHOOD

1. Even though Paul rejoices in his sufferings, he acknowledges the toil and struggle of his ministry. What can you notice about the nature of this toil and struggle (Col. 1:27–2:1)?

2. Paul struggles not only toward his goal but also against the falsehoods threatening to get in the way. Take a moment to review the background of false teachings presented in the introduction. Paul takes these false teachings and turns them on their heads with the truth of the gospel. For your study today, examine how Paul is already beginning to do this (Col. 1:24–2:5). Write down words and phrases that Paul may have been aiming against these false teachings, and briefly comment on them.

Day Four—Paul's Example for Us

1. We must begin to think about what Paul's example means to us. Let's work backwards, starting with these false teachings and the way in which Paul came at them. What sorts of false ideas or teachings today might tend to pull believers away from "walking in him"?

2. How can Paul's example teach us to recognize and deal with any such untruth? Look again through the verses we have studied so far as you consider this question.

3. Consider Paul's example of toiling, struggling, and working hard as a servant of the gospel. How does this challenge and encourage you? Look ahead to Colossians 3:23–24.

4. A related question: What kind of glory are you after? Do you really believe in the mystery that is Christ in you, the hope of glory? How much do you believe 2 Corinthians 4:16–18? Just think on this question, jotting down ideas, questions, or phrases you might want to think on some more.

DAY FIVE—MORE OF PAUL'S EXAMPLE FOR US

Paul offers a challenging example! He hands us hard, soul-searching questions, but they're the ones that really matter.

1. Consider Paul's commission to proclaim Christ, making the word of God fully known—to all the nations. How much was that a special apostolic commission, and how much does it apply to each of us as believers? Look briefly ahead to Colossians 4:2—6: what was the role of the Christians in Colossae, as Paul explained it? Then, too, recall Acts 1:7—8.

2. What about Paul's participation in Christ's afflictions as he boldly delivered the good news—and suffered greatly for it? Thousands in our world today are suffering and dying as they carry the gospel of Christ. How do we regard them? Do we . . . would we count it joy to suffer in carrying the gospel . . . for the sake of Christ's own body, the ones he died to save? What are your thoughts?

3. Enough questions! Look back again through this week's lesson, consider Paul's example, and pick one key verse to think and pray about—and perhaps memorize.

Notes for Lesson 4

Lesson 5 (Col. 2:6–23)

So Then . . . Getting to the Application

Day One—The Main Thing

1. We've arrived at our theme verses, at the beginning of this week's passage. They reach back (as we've seen what it means to receive and proclaim Jesus as Lord) and ahead (as we shall see more clearly how to walk in him). Take time to memorize Colossians 2:6–7, if you haven't already, and say these verses aloud a few times.

2. Make some kind of an outline or picture of these two verses, taking account of each of the five phrases. Be as creative or as uncreative as you wish!

DAY TWO—
WHAT SHAPE WILL THESE WARNINGS TAKE?

1. Now Paul gets to the "walk in him" part, and he begins
   with some clear warnings. We will attempt, first, to get
   the shape of Colossians 2:8–23. Examine the following
   suggested outline, and fill in the blanks according to what
   you see in the text. It's not the only possible outline for
   this passage; you are welcome to construct another.

   I.   Verse 8: Summary Warning

   II. Verses 9–15: _____

        _____

   III. Verses 16–19: Consequent Specific Warning
        1. Verses 16–17: _____

           _____

        2. Verses 18–19: _____

           _____

   IV. Verses 20–23: Summary Warning Reiterated
        Strongly

42

2a. Write down everything Colossians 2:8 tells us about the kind of philosophy we should reject.

b. Is such philosophy around today? Where might you meet it?

DAY THREE—OUR IDENTIFICATION WITH CHRIST

Colossians 2:9–15 reminds us of what has happened to free us from bondage to any worldly philosophies. (*Warning: This is the longest day in the whole study. Save time!*)

1. What are the two huge assertions of Colossians 2:9–10a? As you write, underline the words that stand out to you, and then briefly explain why.

2. The last phrase of Colossians 2:10 tells us something about this Christ whose fullness we share. Why is this phrase important at this point?

3. The passage goes on to show how we through faith participate in the death and resurrection of Christ. Let's start with his death. The hard part about this concept is that we started out dead: how does Colossians 2:13 talk about our spiritual deadness? (Note: Circumcision was the Old Testament practice of cutting off the foreskin of all males in Israel, as a covenant sign that they belonged to God's people.)

4. Paul talks about a different kind of circumcision, one accomplished at the cross. There Christ died in our place, when we were already dead and could not die ourselves to pay for our sins. In what way is this circumcision different from the physical circumcision,

according to Colossians 2:11? See Romans 2:28–29 for further clarification.

5. Colossians 2:12 unfolds the last phrase of verse 11, explaining the circumcision accomplished by Christ. According to Colossians 2:12, how did the Colossians and all believers receive this new circumcision done by Christ? (Note: The answer has two parts.)

Romans 6:1–11 further explains being baptized into Jesus' death and being raised with him to newness of life.

6. In Christ we die, and in Christ we are made alive. Salvation is the work of God, accomplished for us in Christ. Write down all the things done by God, according to Colossians 2:12–15.

7. Colossians 2:14 explains the last phrase of verse 13 with a powerful picture. Describe that picture briefly.

8. Colossians 2:15 uses another vivid picture, that of a victor in war displaying his captives or trophies, often in a triumphal procession. Read Ephesians 6:12 to understand these "rulers and authorities" better, and then explain what Colossians 2:15 says happened to them, and how.

9. We know that Christ has conquered Satan and his evil cohorts through his death and resurrection, but we also know that these evil ones are not yet put away forever. How do we live, in the meantime? What two little words that appear together multiple times in Colossians 2:6–15 offer the answer here? Find several examples, and comment briefly.

Day Four—Therefore . . .

1. What is the "therefore" at the beginning of Colossians 2:16 there for?

2. Study Colossians 2:16–19 carefully. Using the following outline, identify as clearly as possible the two kinds of false teachings threatening the Colossians, and then explain the way each is refuted by the truth of Christ. Finally, suggest possible applications that come to mind.

a. Verses 16–17 ("Let no one _____
    _____ you. . . .")

    • The false teaching:

    • The refutation:

b. Verses 18–19 ("Let no one _____
    _____ you. . . .")

    • The false teaching:

    • The refutation:

c. Possible applications:

DAY FIVE—REMEMBER THE WARNING!

1. As Paul concludes this passage with a sort of summary scolding, he reminds the Colossians that "with Christ you died to the elemental spirits of the world" (Col. 2:20). Can you summarize what he means by this? To what parts of this chapter would you return to help explain?

2. Colossians 2:21–23 offers a final warning against regulations based simply on human precepts and teachings. According to these verses, what are the various drawbacks of such regulations?

3. What tempts you to act "as though you still belonged" to the world and its basic principles?

4. Paul does not urge us simply to believe accurately about Christ, does he? Nor does he urge us simply to act rightly. He puts these two urgings together in an amazing way. How? Read one more time through Colossians 2:6–23, recalling key words and phrases, as you muse on this question for yourself.

Notes for Lesson 5

Lesson 6 (Col. 3:1–4)

FOUR SHORT AND
WEIGHTY VERSES

In Colossians 2:20, we read, "If with Christ you died..."—and we saw in Colossians 2 the principles of this world we should "die to." Now, Colossians 3 begins, "If then you have been raised with Christ...." In these verses, Paul tries to complete the whole picture of our identification with Christ.

To make our way through this book and get a sense of its whole message, we have been moving through significant chunks in each lesson. This week, however, let's slow down. We will practice a more concentrated study method, focusing on only four verses—one each day, after the first day's introduction. These four verses will indeed take a lifetime to comprehend and obey, but let us begin in this lesson to take them to heart.

DAY ONE—TAKE THEM IN

1. Read Colossians 3:1–4 several times. Memorize these verses, if you haven't already. They will reward you!

2. As you examine these verses carefully, write down your initial observations and questions.

DAY TWO—COLOSSIANS 3:1

1. We know that we will be raised with Christ in the final resurrection of the dead. But think again about what it means, now, to have been raised with Christ. What do the following passages add to your understanding?

• Ephesians 2:4–7

• Romans 6:1–13

2. Write your own summary statement of what it means to have been raised with Christ.

3a. The logical result of being raised with Christ follows in the rest of Colossians 3:1. How might you get off track if you tried to understand the middle phrase ("seek the things that are above") by itself?

b. How does the third and final phrase tell us what Paul means by "things above"?

c. Meditate on the reality of that scene above. Read Hebrews 10:11–14 and Acts 7:54–56.

4a. The main command of Colossians 3:1 literally reads not "set your hearts," but rather, "keep seeking." How would you explain what it means to "keep seeking the things above"?

b. Why can we obey this command only if we have been raised with Christ?

DAY THREE—COLOSSIANS 3:2

1. Examine each phrase of Colossians 3:2: in what important ways does Paul here further develop and clarify the command of verse 1?

2. Can you think of some specific examples of "minding" earthly things, as opposed to "things above"?

3. According to 1 Timothy 6:17–19, what should be the set of our minds toward earthly things and toward things above?

Day Four—Colossians 3:3

1. The opening of Colossians 3:3 reminds us why we cannot set our minds on earthly things. Look back through lesson 5, day 3, and then consider Galatians 2:20a. What is important to say about these first startling words of Colossians 3:3?

2. Of course you cannot read just the first part of Galatians 2:20, any more than you can read just the first part of Colossians 3:3! If we are in Christ, why do the first parts of these verses necessarily imply the second parts?

3. None of us could ever sum up what this beautiful second phrase of Colossians 3:3 means. Knowing that, think through each word carefully, and try to write down some of what it means for your life to be "hidden with Christ in God."

4a. "Hidden" implies "safe and secure," but it also implies "invisible." What does the fact that our "life" is "invisible" mean for us now?

b. How do the following verses help us with this concept of our presently invisible life?

- 2 Corinthians 4:18

- Hebrews 11:1

- Hebrews 12:2

DAY FIVE—COLOSSIANS 3:4

With Colossians 3:4, we get to the hope of the resurrection to come! Our life, now hidden (Col. 3:3), will burst into full view with the appearing of Christ, "who is our life."

1. Don't you like to know what's going to happen in advance? On the day of his appearing, according to 1 Thessalonians 4:13–18:

   a.   What will Jesus do?

   b.   What will happen to believers who have already died ("fallen asleep")?

   c.   What will happen to believers who are alive at that time?

2. What more do you learn about this appearing, in 2 Thessalonians 1:6–10?

3. Glory can be defined as "God's holy being fully shining forth." What will it mean for us to appear with Christ in glory? Before writing your answer, read 1 Corinthians 15:51–52 and 1 John 3:2. Read 1 Corinthians 15: 12–58 if you have time.

4a. Write the "with . . ." phrases from Colossians 2:20, 3:1, 3:3, and 3:4. Consider: Do these phrases describe the shape of your life?

b. Meditate on John 17:24 and Revelation 21:3.

5. What better verses to encourage our hearts to walk in him faithfully until that day! If you have received Christ Jesus as Lord, tell yourself Colossians 3:1–4 one more time, with the great confidence that comes from "Christ in you, the hope of glory."

Notes on Lesson 6

Lesson 7 (*Col. 3:5–14*)

FULL-SCALE APPLICATION

Colossians 2 began to apply the grand truths about Christ taught in the first part of this book. But we did keep getting wonderfully pulled up into thoughts about Christ and "things above." May our minds and hearts be continually pulled above like this, to Christ—and, as a result, we will properly see and live our lives. Such a result is what Paul is addressing in this week's passage.

DAY ONE—THE PASSAGE AS A WHOLE

1. Read Colossians 3:5–14. What would you say is the main idea of this section?

2. How does this section relate to the theme verses (Col. 2:6–7)?

3. Study the shape and organization of these verses. How would you divide them up, and why?

DAY TWO—THE OLD SELF (COL. 3:5–9)

1. What is the "therefore" in Colossians 3:5 there for?

2. What two imperatives (commands) does Paul give in relation to the old, earthly self and its practices? Read Colossians 3:5, 8.

3. What is true about this old, earthly self and its practices? Read Colossians 3:6–7, 9.

4a. In Colossians 3:5, look at the list of evils we must put to death. What can you observe about this grouping?

b. How does the world around us often encourage these evils?

c. Why is <u>covetousness idolatry</u>?

5a. What characteristics of the list in Colossians 3:8 do you notice?

b. Where can we meet these evils today?

c. Colossians 3:9 adds, "Do not lie to one another."
Why do you think Paul highlights this command so
prominently?

6. Now look back at both lists, in Colossians 3:5 and
Colossians 3:8. What are some ways we can specifically
and actively "put to death" and "rid ourselves of" these
evils? Don't forget the first four verses of this chapter.

DAY THREE—THE NEW SELF (COL. 3:10-12)

1. Write down everything we can know about this "new
self," according to Colossians 3:10.

2. What do we know about our "new self," according to the following verses?

- 2 Corinthians 5:17

- 2 Corinthians 3:18

3. Colossians 3:11 reminds us that Paul is addressing a church, a group of believers. The evils we've seen do reside within individual hearts, but they are evils that also reach out and destroy others. The false teachings Paul combats in this letter were encouraging such evils through harmful sensual license and through the other extreme of divisive legalism. By contrast, Paul describes the new creation of the body of Christ as unified, bound together in love. According to Colossians 3:11, what barriers does he say have been broken down, and why? (Note: "Barbarian" refers to a non-Greek-speaking and therefore "uncivilized" person. "Scythian" refers to an

inhabitant of northern Greece, considered uncouth and uncultured by most other Greeks.)

4. What kinds of barriers must the people of God deal with today?

5a. In Colossians 3:12, what initial descriptions of the body of Christ does Paul use to address this body of believers?

b. Read Deuteronomy 7:6–8, and find in this Old Testament description of Israel the seeds of Paul's terminology in Colossians 3:12: "God's chosen ones, holy and beloved." What can you learn from seeing this continuity in God's dealing with his people? See the conclusion in Deuteronomy 7:9.

DAY FOUR—NEW CLOTHES (COL. 3:12–14)

1. What image does Paul use in the command of Colossians 3:12? See Colossians 3:9–10 as well. How is this language more helpful than simply, "Be compassionate," or "Be kind"?

2a. What can you observe about the list of new clothes (Col. 3:12)?

b. How does Colossians 3:13 offer great help in learning how to put on such a wardrobe?

c. In what particular situations can you work on obeying this command to bear with one another? How about the command to forgive as the Lord has forgiven you?

3a. What part of the wardrobe is love, and why? See Colossians 3:14.

b. What characterizes this love in the body of Christ, according to Colossians 1:3–8?

DAY FIVE—
THINKING ABOUT HOW WE'RE DRESSED

In conclusion, let's stand back and think on this vivid picture of what it looks like for those who have received Christ Jesus as Lord to walk in him: it looks like a change of clothes! How do the following verses remind us and instruct us about this change?

1. Isaiah 61:10

2. 2 Corinthians 5:21

3. Romans 13:11–14

4. Revelation 19:6–8 (This passage records John's vision of the glory to come, when Jesus will gather all his people to be with him forever.)

Notes for Lesson 7

Lesson 8 (Col. 3:15–4:1)

APPLICATION THAT HITS HOME

DAY ONE—
UPLIFTING DIRECTION (COL. 3:15-17)

1. We have received quite a challenging picture of what our new clothing in Christ is to look like. The Lord knows we need encouragement and direction as we aim to obey. Naturally, that encouragement focuses largely on our hearts. Study the first sentence of Colossians 3:15, and write down everything you observe about the peace to which God's people are called.

2. Carefully study Colossians 3:16, and write down everything you observe about taking in God's Word. All the following phrases support and relate to that first admonition about the word of Christ.

3a. Colossians 3:17 sums it all up. What does it mean to do something "in the name of" someone else?

b. What does it mean to do everything in the name of the Lord Jesus?

c. What previous passages might help here?

4. Notice how beautifully these three verses (Col. 3:15–17) hold together.

   a. How is Christ central to each one?

   b. How does thankfulness flow out of each one?

   c. What part of these encouragements do you most need to hear, and why?

DAY TWO—HOUSEHOLD RULES (COL. 3:18–4:1)

Living with the new clothes and according to the directions set forth in Colossians 3:5–17 will affect every action and interaction. We "walk in him" through every single part of our lives. In these verses, Paul sets forth what was commonly known as a set of household rules.

1. What pattern(s) of organization do you find in these six rules (Col. 3:18–4:1)?

2a. Can you determine one main principle, relative to the Lord Jesus Christ, that Paul is trying to apply to all these different relationships?

b. How does this main principle fit in with the main theme of Colossians?

3. Paul's instructions here are quick, short summaries of instructions given more fully elsewhere. Why do you think he gives these commands in this way here?

DAY THREE—WIVES AND HUSBANDS

1. "Wives, submit"—and here we have a plain, simple command that somehow opens a huge can of worms! We will not cover this issue in depth here, as Paul does not, but we can ask key questions and take in clear truth. First, the command to submit, which means to acknowledge and respect an authority, comes with what significant commentary (Col. 3:18)? What does that added phrase mean?

2. God has created order but not bondage or inferiority. What clarification do you find in Galatians 3:26–28 and 1 Corinthians 11:3?

3a. In Colossians 3:19, how do the one positive command and the one negative command to husbands show, in a nutshell, the kind of headship Paul is advocating?

b. Out of all possible negative qualities, why do you think Paul picks harshness?

4. These commands called for a marriage relationship quite radical in Paul's day. Are these verses radical in our day as well? Explain.

5. To all, married and not: In what ways is it important for you to understand clearly what God intended for husbands and wives?

DAY FOUR—
CHILDREN AND PARENTS; SLAVES AND MASTERS

1. Consider the command to children in Colossians 3:20. According to this verse, for what reason should children obey their parents? How can we communicate both this command and this reason to children?

2a. What might surprise you about Colossians 3:21, especially by contrast?

  b. How might a father "provoke" or "exasperate" his children (Col. 3:21)?

c. What might you observe about the reason given here?

d. Why do you think Paul addresses only fathers? Does this apply to mothers as well?

3. How are the commands to slaves and masters different from the others so far? Read Colossians 3:22–4:1.

4. In what similar and different ways should the presence of a heavenly master change the perspective of both a slave and a master?

5. Look and see how many times the Lord is mentioned in Colossians 3:22–4:1. How must we as Christians let our Lord Jesus Christ more directly affect the way we work—and the way we supervise the work of others? How does this question apply to you? Remember Galatians 3:26–28.

6. Why do you think Paul does not preach here the immediate abolition of slavery? Remember Galatians 3:26–28.

7. Now turn to the parallel and much more developed passage in Ephesians 5:22–6:9. Write down just three or four out of many possible clarifications and explanations that help you better understand the passage in Colossians. (Note: The passage in Ephesians is a great one to come back to for further study.)

DAY FIVE—THINKING AND PRAYING

Paul has set forth a relationship with the Lord Jesus Christ that radically affects all our other relationships—with those at church, at home, at work—and, as we shall see next week, with "outsiders" as well. Think through your various networks of relationships, and ask God to show you how you can more faithfully obey his word and honor his name in each one. Use Colossians 3:17 to write your own final prayer for this week.

Notes for Lesson 8

Lesson 9 (Col. 4:2–18)

THE PEOPLE AROUND US

DAY ONE—"OUTSIDERS" (COL. 4:2-6)

We've learned about our new clothes—in Christ—and we've been told just how to wear them, in all kinds of particular contexts, as we saw last week. The last context Paul touches is that of "outsiders" (Col. 4:5): the people who do not yet know Jesus Christ as Savior and Lord.

1. Why do you think this section comes last, in this whole list of relational directions?

2. How would you organize or outline Colossians 4:2–6?

3. Prayer is clearly the first step in evangelism, according to these verses. Meditate a bit on Colossians 4:2, and then write down each important word and your brief thoughts concerning it.

4. Colossians 4:3–4 gives us the first responsibility of praying for those who preach the gospel. Write a list of Paul's prayer requests. What do these requests tell us about Paul's attitude toward the gospel of Jesus Christ?

5. Colossians 4:5–6 gives church members their own responsibility to tell the gospel. How is this responsibility different from that of one called to preach?

6. What do you think it means for our speech always to be "gracious" and "seasoned with salt"? Can you think of any examples?

DAY TWO—STOP, THINK, AND PRAY

Look back through the Scripture and questions from day 1. Using what you find there, write a list of prayer requests—asking God, in specific ways, to help you do what those verses command. Take time to pray. Pray that God will help you to pray. Be watchful and thankful in your prayers! How amazing that we can go to God, through Christ, and talk to him about what he is telling us in his Word.

DAY THREE—WHO'S WHO (COL. 4:7–18)

1. Paul reveals an amazing network of relationships in his final greetings. For each of the following names, write what you know from Colossians and from other references mentioned.

   a. Tychicus (Col. 4:7–8; Acts 20:4; Eph. 6:21–22)

   b. Onesimus (Col. 4:9; Philem. 8–21)

   c. Aristarchus (Col. 4:10–11; Acts 19:29; 20:4; 27:2)

d. Mark (Col. 4:10–11; Acts 15:36–40; 2 Tim. 4:11)

e. Justus (Col. 4:11)

f. Epaphras (Col. 4:12–13; 1:7–8; Philem. 23)

g. Luke (Col. 4:14; Luke 1:1–4; Acts 16:10, where Luke is part of "we"; 2 Tim. 4:11)

h. Demas (Col. 4:14; 2 Tim. 4:10)

i. Nympha (Col. 4:15)

j. Archippus (Col. 4:17; Philem. 2)

2. Now, look over the list of names again. What observations can you make concerning Paul's relationships and his way of speaking about them?

3. In what ways does this glimpse into Paul's network of relationships challenge your own?

DAY FOUR—WHAT PAUL HAS LEFT US

1. Comment on the significance of what Paul says about Epaphras in Colossians 4:12–13

    a. as a fitting conclusion to Paul's various comments on prayer in this letter.

    b. as a final corrective to the false teachings of which Epaphras has informed him and that Paul has addressed in this letter.

2. How do Paul and others evidently regard what he has written?

a. Colossians 4:16

b. 1 Thessalonians 5:27

c. Acts 22:12−15

d. 2 Peter 3:15−16

3. In the final section, Paul ceases dictating and takes the pen in his own hand to give his personal greeting and authority to this letter. What does Paul want to leave with his readers by means of his two, short closing statements?

DAY FIVE—LOOKING BACK

1. Look back to Paul's main purpose in writing to Christ's church (Col. 2:2–3; see also lesson 1, day 4). In what ways has this purpose been accomplished in you as you have studied Paul's words?

2. Look back to or recite by memory what we have called the book's theme verses, Colossians 2:6–7. These verses give a command. In what ways has Paul's letter to the Colossians helped equip you to obey that command?

3. Now, do one final look-through of this great epistle we have studied, stopping to offer thanksgiving and petitions to God as you make your way, one more time, through these words he has inspired.

Notes for Lesson 9

Lesson 10 (Philemon)

PERSONAL STUDY OF A
PERSONAL LETTER

In our study of Colossians, we have been practicing the Bible study methods listed in this study's introduction. Now, with another of Paul's epistles written at the same time, you have the opportunity to practice these methods on your own. The steps presented in the introduction have been divided up into five days' work, but you may want to adjust your schedule according to your own pace. As you have observed, the methods and the order of the methods are not inflexible; we must ask the questions and make the observations that the text itself demands. May God, through his Spirit, open up this lovely little book to our hearts and minds as we study.

Philemon, a Christian in Colossae, had a slave named Onesimus, who ran away . . . only to meet up with Paul—and Christ. Along with Tychicus and the letter to all the Colossians, Paul sent Onesimus and this letter back to Philemon.

DAY ONE—READ AND OBSERVE

DAY TWO—STARTING TO ASK QUESTIONS

1. Why is this text here?

    a. In other words, identify the main point, or *theme*, of the book.

    b. Look for a *theme verse* or verses that capture the book's main point.

2. Why does it say what it says in the way it says it?

    a. Consider first the *original recipients* of the book and how they would have understood it.

b. Examine the book's *organization*, or shape: How do the different parts work together to support the main theme?

c. Find *key words* and determine their meaning and significance in the book.

d. Observe the book's *literary style* and the way in which that style contributes to the meaning.

DAY THREE—ASKING MORE QUESTIONS

3a. How does this text point us to Jesus?

b. Discover how this book supports and develops the *Bible's main theme* of God's redeeming a people through Jesus Christ for his own glory.

4. What are the surprises in this book?

a. Continually look to *notice* and *learn* what you didn't know or expect.

5a. What is the application?

b. Identify *specific personal applications.*

DAY FOUR—STUDYING SHORTER SECTIONS

Pick one or two sections within the book to study in more detail, asking as many as possible of the following questions.

1. What is the main idea here?

2. What questions does the text make me ask?

3. How does this section connect with verses before and after?

4. How is this section organized?

5. What key words do I find?

6. How does this section support the book's main theme?

7. What other Scriptures shed crucial light on these verses?

8. How does this section apply to me?

Day Five—Looking Back

You may have some work left to finish today. After completing your study, look back over the book and over the work you've done. Write down what you'd like to remember about Philemon and about studying a book of the Bible.

Notes for Lesson 10

NOTES FOR LEADERS

What a privilege it is to lead a group in studying the Word of God! Following are six principles offered to help guide you as you lead.

1. THE PRIMACY OF THE BIBLICAL TEXT

If you forget all the other principles, I encourage you to hold on to this one! The Bible is God speaking to us, through his inspired Word—living and active and sharper than a two-edged sword. As leaders, we aim to point people as effectively as possible into this Word. We can trust the Bible to do all that God intends in the lives of those studying with us.

This means that the job of a leader is to direct the conversation of a group constantly back into the text. If you "get stuck," usually the best thing to say is: "Let's go back to the text and read it again. . . ." The questions in this study aim to lead people into the text, rather than into a swirl of personal opinions about the topics of the text; therefore, depending on the questions should help. Personal opinions and experiences will often enrich your group's interactions; however, many Bible studies these days have moved almost exclusively into the realm of "What does this mean to me?" rather than first trying to get straight on "What does this mean?"

We'll never understand the text perfectly, but we can stand on one of the great principles of the Reformation: the *perspicuity* of Scripture. This simply means *understandability*. God made us word-creatures, in his image, and he gave us a Word that he means us to understand—more and more—with careful reading, study, shared counsel, and prayer.

The primacy of the text implies less of a dependence on commentaries and answer guides than often has been the case. I do not offer answers to the questions, because the answers are in the biblical text, and we desperately need to learn how to dig in and find them. When individuals articulate what they find for themselves (leaders included!), they have learned more, with each of their answers, about studying God's Word. These competencies are then transferable and applicable in every other study of the Bible. Without a set of answers, a leader will not be an "answer person," but rather a fellow searcher of the Scriptures.

Helps *are* helpful in the right place! It is good to keep at hand a Bible dictionary of some kind. The lessons themselves actually offer context and help with the questions as they are asked. A few commentaries are listed in the "Notes on Translations and Study Helps," and these can give further guidance after one has spent good time with the text itself. I place great importance as well on the help of leaders and teachers in one's church, which leads us into the second principle.

2. THE CONTEXT OF THE CHURCH

As Christians, we have a new identity: we are part of the body of Christ. According to the New Testament, that body is clearly meant to live and work in local bodies, local churches. The ideal context for Bible study is within a church body—one that is reaching out in all directions to the people around it. (Bible studies can be the best places for evangelism!) I realize that these studies will be used in all kinds of ways and places; but whatever the context, I would hope that the group leaders have a layer of solid church leaders around them, people to whom they can go with questions and concerns as they study the Scriptures. When a leader doesn't know the answer to a question that arises, it's really OK to say, "I don't know. But I'll be happy to try to find out." Then that leader can go to pastors and teachers, as well as to commentaries, in order to learn more.

The church context has many ramifications for Bible study. For example, when a visitor attends a study and comes to know the Lord, the visitor—and his or her family—can be plugged into the context of the church. For another example, what happens in a Bible study often can be integrated with other courses of study within the church, and even with the preaching, so that the whole body learns and grows together. This depends, of course, on the connection of those leading the study with those leading the church—a connection that I have found to be most fruitful and encouraging.

3. THE IMPORTANCE OF PLANNING AND THINKING AHEAD

How many of us have experienced the rush to get to Bible study on time . . . or have jumped in without thinking through what will happen during the precious minutes of group interaction . . . or have felt out of control as we've made our way through a quarter of the questions and used up three-quarters of the time!

It is crucial, after having worked through the lesson yourself, to think it through from the perspective of leading the discussion. How will you open the session, giving perhaps a nutshell statement of the main theme and the central goals for the day? (Each lesson offers a brief introduction that will help with the opening.) Which questions do you not want to miss discussing, and which ones could you quickly summarize or even skip? How much time would you like to allot for the different sections of the study?

If you're leading a group by yourself, you will need to prepare extra carefully—and that can be done! If you're part of a larger study, perhaps with multiple small groups, it's helpful for the various group leaders to meet together and to help each other with the planning. Often, a group of leaders meets early on the morning of a study in order to help the others with the fruit of their study, plan the group time, and pray—which leads into the fourth principle.

4. THE CRUCIAL ROLE OF PRAYER

If these words we're studying are truly the inspired Word of God, then how much we need to ask for his Spirit's help and guidance as we study his revelation! This is a prayer found often in Scripture itself, and a prayer God evidently loves to answer: that he would give us understanding of his truth, according to his Word. I encourage you as a leader to pray before and as you work through the lesson, to encourage those in your group to do the same, to model this kind of prayer as you lead the group time, to pray for your group members by name throughout the week, and to ask one or two "prayer warriors" in your life to pray for you as you lead.

5. THE SENSITIVE ART OF LEADING

Whole manuals, of course, have been written on this subject! Actually, the four principles preceding this one may be most fundamental in cultivating your group leadership ability. Again, I encourage you to consider yourself not as a person with all the right answers, but rather as one who studies along with the people in your group—and who then facilitates the group members' discussion of all they have discovered in the Scriptures.

There is always a tension between pouring out the wisdom of all your own preparation and knowledge, on the one hand,

and encouraging those in your group to relish and share all they have learned, on the other. I advise leaders to lean more heavily toward the latter, reserving the former to steer gently and wisely through a well-planned group discussion. What we're trying to accomplish is not to cement our own roles as leaders, but to participate in God's work of raising up mature Christians who know how to study and understand the Word—and who will themselves become equipped to lead.

With specific issues in group leading—such as encouraging everybody to talk, or handling one who talks too much—I encourage you to seek the counsel of one with experience in leading groups. There is no better help than the mentoring and prayerful support of a wise person who has been there! That's even better than the best "how-to" manual. If you have a number of group leaders, perhaps you will invite an experienced group leader to come and conduct a practical session on how to lead.

Remember: the default move is, "Back to the text!"

6. The Power of the Scriptures to Delight

Finally, in the midst of it all, let us not forget to delight together in the Scriptures! We should be serious but not joyless! In fact, we as leaders should model for our groups a growing and satisfying delight in the Word of God—as we notice its beauty, stop to linger over a lovely word or phrase, enjoy the poetry, appreciate the shape of a passage from beginning to end, laugh at a touch of irony or an image that hits home, wonder over a truth that pierces the soul.

May we share and spread the response of Jeremiah, who said:

> Your words were found, and I ate them,
>   and your words became to me a joy
>   and the delight of my heart. (Jer. 15:16)

117

General Outline
of Colossians

The following represents the large shape of the book, which you will discover and develop in more detail for yourself, through the course of the study.

Warning: Do not read this outline until you have completed Lesson One!

I. Introduction (1:1-14)

Theological foundation, personally presented:
II. All about Jesus (1:15-23)
III. From the heart of Paul (1:24–2:5)

The Hinge of the Book:
from the delivery of truth
to the application of that truth (2:6-7)

Application of theological truth:
IV. Walking in him. . . How? (2:8–23)
V. Death and Life Acted Out (3:1–4:6)

VI. Conclusion: Loving Greetings (4:7-18)

SUGGESTED MEMORY PASSAGES

Therefore, as you received Christ Jesus the Lord, so walk in him, rooted and built up in him and established in the faith, just as you were taught, abounding in thanksgiving.

Colossians 2:6–7

If then you have been raised with Christ, seek the things that are above, where Christ is seated at the right hand of God. Set your minds on things that are above, not on things that are on earth. For you have died, and your life is hidden with Christ in God. When Christ who is your life appears, then you also will appear with him in glory.

Colossians 3:1–4

And let the peace of Christ rule in your hearts, to which indeed you were called in one body. And be thankful. Let the word of Christ dwell in you richly, teaching and admonishing one another in all wisdom, singing psalms and hymns and spiritual songs, with thankfulness in your hearts to God. And whatever you do, in word or deed, do everything in the name of the Lord Jesus, giving thanks to God the Father through him.

Colossians 3:15–17

Notes on Translations and Study Helps

This study can be done with any reliable translation of the Bible, although I recommend the English Standard Version for its essentially literal but beautifully readable translation of the original languages. In preparing this study, I have used and quoted from the English Standard Version, published by Crossway Bibles in Wheaton, Illinois.

These lessons are designed to be completed with only the Bible open in front of you. The point is to grapple with the text, not with what others have said about the text. The goal is to know, increasingly, the joy and reward of digging into the Scriptures, God's breathed-out words that are not only able to make us wise for salvation through faith in Christ Jesus but also profitable for teaching, reproof, correction, and training in righteousness, that each of us may be competent, equipped for every good work (2 Tim. 3:15–17). To help you dig in, basic and helpful contexts and comments are given throughout the lessons. I have used and learned from the following books in my study and preparation; you may find sources such as these helpful at some point.

NOTES ON TRANSLATIONS AND STUDY HELPS

GENERAL HANDBOOKS

The Crossway Comprehensive Concordance of the Holy Bible: English Standard Version. Compiled by William D. Mounce. Wheaton, IL: Crossway Books, 2002. (Other concordances are available, from various publishers and for different translations.)

The Illustrated Bible Dictionary. 4 vols. Wheaton, IL: Tyndale House Publishers, 1980. (*The Zondervan Pictorial Encyclopedia of the Bible* is similarly helpful.)

Ryken, Leland, James Wilhoit, and Tremper Longman III, eds. *Dictionary of Biblical Imagery.* Downers Grove, IL: InterVarsity Press, 1998.

Ryken, Leland, Philip Ryken, and James Wilhoit. *Ryken's Bible Handbook.* Wheaton, IL: Tyndale House Publishers, 2005.

Vine's Complete Expository Dictionary of Old and New Testament Words. Nashville: Thomas Nelson, 1984.

COMMENTARIES

Hughes, R. Kent. *Colossians and Philemon: The Supremacy of Christ.* Wheaton, IL: Crossway Books, 1989.

Jensen, Phillip D., and Tony Payne. *Colossians: Continuing in Christ.* Faithwalk Bible Studies. Wheaton, IL: Crossway Books, 1991.

Lightfoot, J. B. *Colossians and Philemon.* Wheaton, IL: Crossway Books, 1997.

Lucas, R. L. *The Message of Colossians and Philemon.* Leicester, England: Inter-Varsity Press, 1980.

O'Brien, P. T. *Colossians and Philemon.* Word Biblical Commentary. Vol. 44. Waco, TX: Word, 1982.

A native of St. Louis, Missouri, **Kathleen Nielson** holds M.A. and Ph.D. degrees in literature from Vanderbilt University and a B.A. from Wheaton College. She has taught in the English departments at Vanderbilt University, Bethel College (Minnesota), and Wheaton College. She is the author of numerous Bible studies and has published two books on biblical poetry, as well as various articles and poems. Kathleen has directed and taught women's Bible studies at several churches, speaks extensively at women's conferences and retreats, and serves on the board of trustees of Wheaton College and on the board of directors of Focus on the Family. Kathleen is married to Dr. Niel Nielson, president of Covenant College in Lookout Mountain, Georgia. Kathleen and Niel have three sons.